English
At Your Command!

HAMPTON-BROWN

Welcome!

This book will help you in school.
Use this book when you need to:

- talk and listen

- make a picture
  of your ideas

- write

- find information.

This book puts
English at Your Command!

Contents

Welcome!

Let's Talk!

Picture It!

Graphic Organizers to

Use Tools and Rules!

Put It in Writing!

The Research Process

Give an Oral Report

1. Think about what you will say.

2. Make notes on cards.

3. Practice your talk.

4. Look at people when you speak.

5. Talk loudly and clearly.

Make It Interesting!

Use details in your report.

✔ Tell what people, places, or things are like.

✔ Tell how they look, sound, feel, smell, or taste.

Tips for Talks

When you talk to a group,
think about these things:

- ✓ **What** is happening?
- ✓ **Who** is listening?
- ✓ **Why** are you talking?
- ✓ **How big** is the group? How loudly do you need to talk?

report

storytime

special day

Details Web

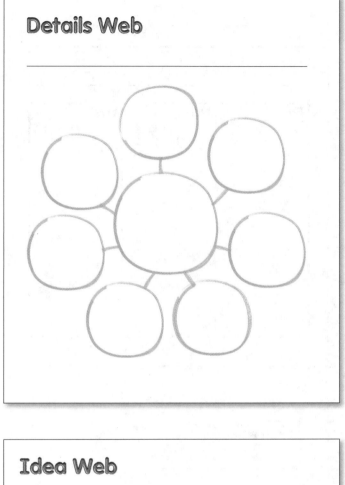

Details Chart

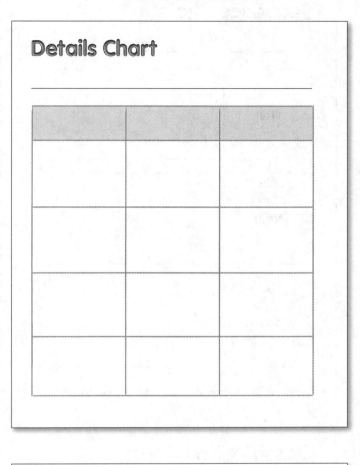

Idea Web

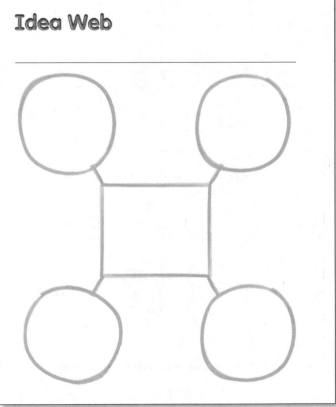

Venn Diagram

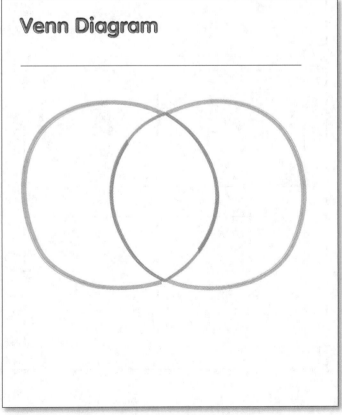

Sequence Chain

First	

↓

Next	

↓

Last	

Sequence Chart

First,	Next,	Last,

Classification Chart

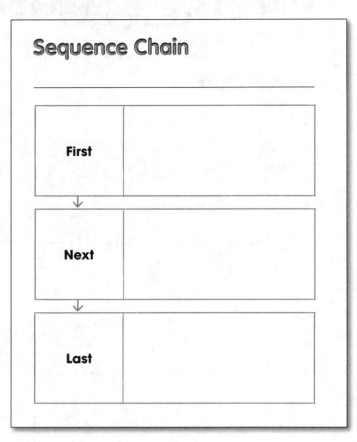

T-Chart

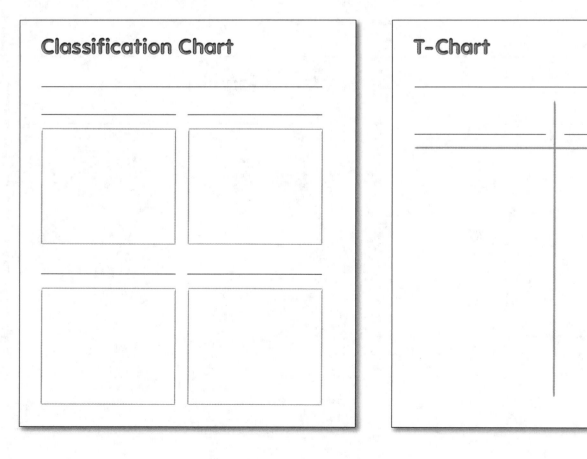

Beginning, Middle, End Map

_____

Beginning

Middle

End

Story Map

_____

_____

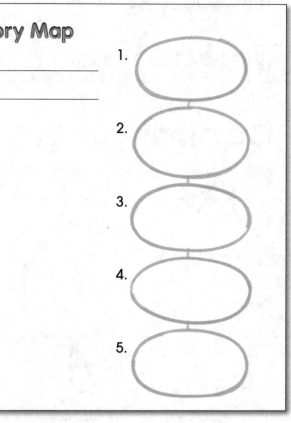

1.

2.

3.

4.

5.

Character Chart

_____

Character	What the Character Does	What This Shows About the Character

Problem-and-Solution Map

_____

Problem:

First:

Next:

Last:

Solution:

Write the Alphabet

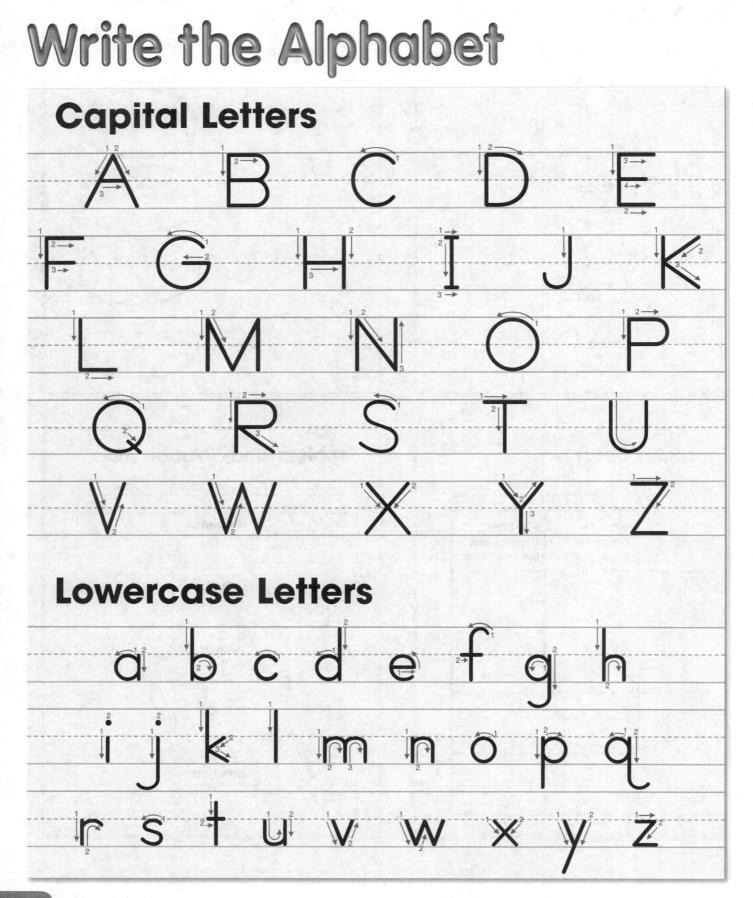

Capital Letters

Lowercase Letters

Handwriting Tips

1. Sit up straight. Keep both feet on the floor.

2. Stay relaxed.

3. Hold your pencil and paper the right way.

If you are left-handed:

If you are right-handed:

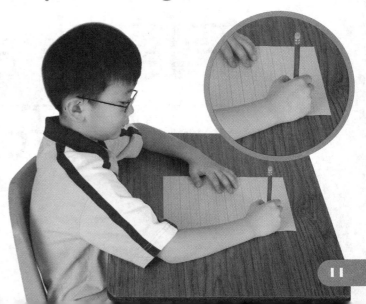

Write Words and Sentences

1. Put a little space between letters.

2. Put more space between words.

3. Write to the end of a line.

Not OK

too close

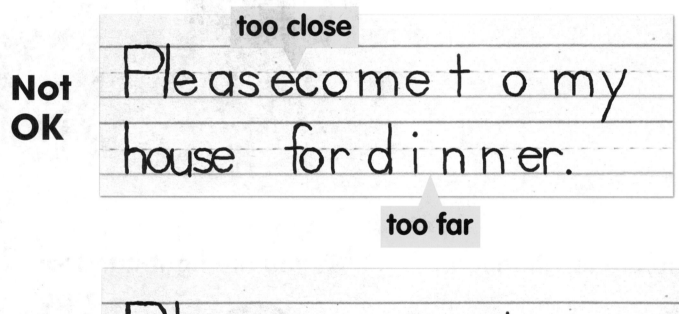

Please come to my house for dinner.

too far

OK

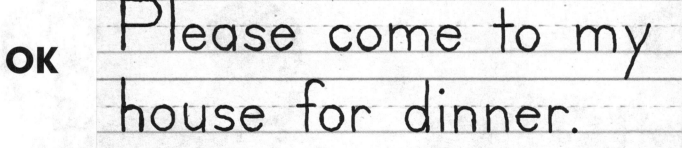

Please come to my house for dinner.

All About Sentences

A sentence has a **naming part** and an **action part** .

Example:

The elephant waves his trunk .

Start a sentence with a **capital letter**. End with an **end mark**.

Examples:

A bat can fly. **period**

Do elephants fly? **question mark**

No, elephants do not fly! **exclamation point**

Words with Capital Letters

Some words name special things.
They start with **capital letters**.

name

title

Dr. Lisa Williams
The Pet Vet
340 Main Street

street name

Spell These Right!

Be a super speller!
Learn these words.

come	the
do	there
does	they
from	to
have	two
live	was
of	were
one	what
said	who
some	you

The Writing Process

STEP 1 Get Ready to Write

- Make a list of **ideas**.

- Choose an idea.

- Decide who your **audience**, or readers, will be.

- Write **details** about your idea. Make a web.

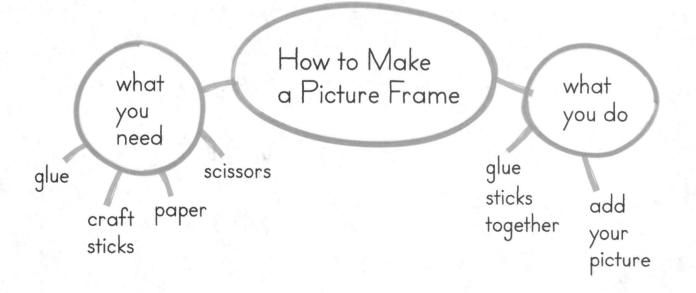

STEP
2 Draft

When you **draft**, you write fast.
Do not worry about mistakes.

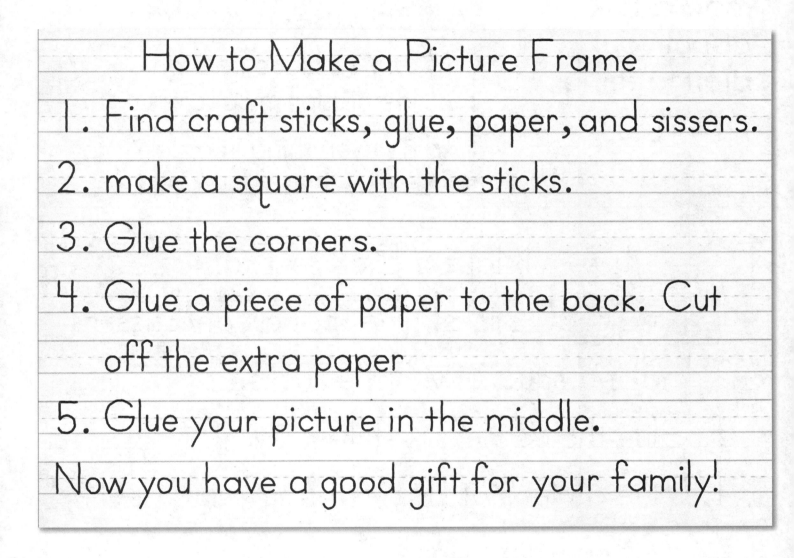

How to Make a Picture Frame

1. Find craft sticks, glue, paper, and sissers.

2. make a square with the sticks.

3. Glue the corners.

4. Glue a piece of paper to the back. Cut off the extra paper

5. Glue your picture in the middle.

Now you have a good gift for your family!

③ Make It Better

Read your draft. Have a partner read it. Talk about your draft together.

Ask these questions:

✓ Did I use good words?

✓ Did I include enough details for my audience?

✓ Is everything in order?

How to Make a Picture Frame

1. Find four^ craft sticks, glue, paper, and sissers.

2. make a square with the sticks.

3. Glue the corners. ^Let them dry.

4. Glue a piece of paper to the back. ^Cut Trim off the extra paper

5. Glue your picture in the middle.

Now you have a special~~good~~ gift for your family!

Use Interesting Words

A **synonym** means almost the same thing as another word. Choose a synonym that tells just what you mean.

big
large
huge
tall

cut
snip
slice
trim

go
move
walk
leave

good
nice
great
special

say
tell
shout
whisper

small
little
tiny
short

4 Check Your Work

Check your spelling and punctuation. Use **proofreading marks**.

Mark	Meaning
∧	Add.
✐	Take out.
≡	Capitalize.
⊙	Add a period.

How to Make a Picture Frame

1. Find ∧craft sticks, glue, paper, and ~~sissers~~. *scissors*.
   four

2. ≡make a square with the sticks.

3. Glue the corners. ∧Let them dry.

4. Glue a piece of paper to the back. ∧~~Cut~~ *Trim* off the extra paper⊙

5. Glue your picture in the middle.

Now you have a ∧~~good~~ *special* gift for your family!

STEP
⑤ Share Your Work

Make a final copy of your work.
Then share it. You can:

- ✓ make a poster
- ✓ make a book
- ✓ read your work to the class
- ✓ e-mail your work to a friend.

How to Make a Picture Frame

1. Find four craft sticks, glue, paper, and scissors.
2. Make a square with the sticks.
3. Glue the corners. Let them dry.
4. Glue a piece of paper to the back. Trim off the extra paper.
5. Glue your picture in the middle.

Now you have a special gift for your family!

Captions and Labels

Captions and **labels** tell about
a picture.

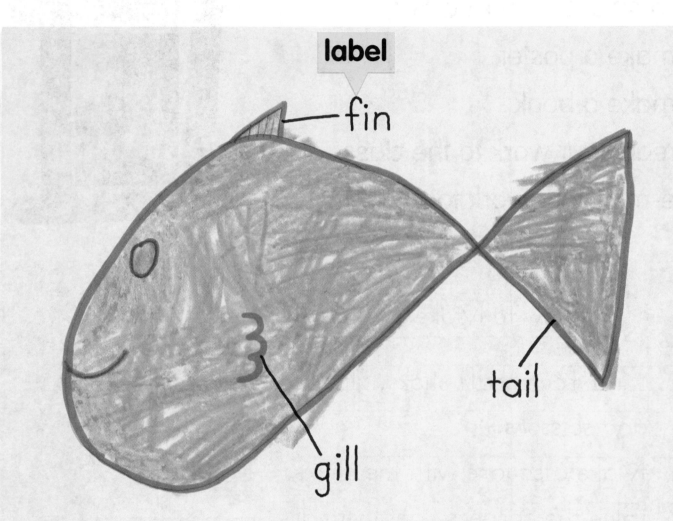

label

fin

tail

gill

caption Fish swim with their
fins and tails.

Chart

A **chart** shows information.

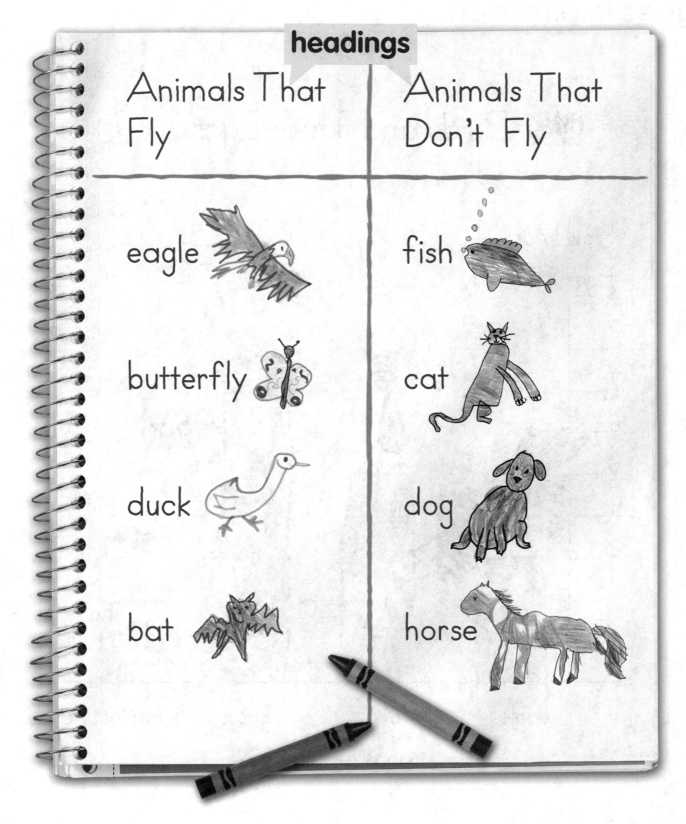

Graph

A **graph** has lines and numbers.
It gives information.

title ▶ Birds and Their Eggs

How Many
Eggs They Lay

bar

8
7
6
5
4
3
2
1
0

eagle   owl   goose   hummingbird

Kinds of Birds

Letters and Notes

Message

A **message** is a short note to someone.
It tells information.

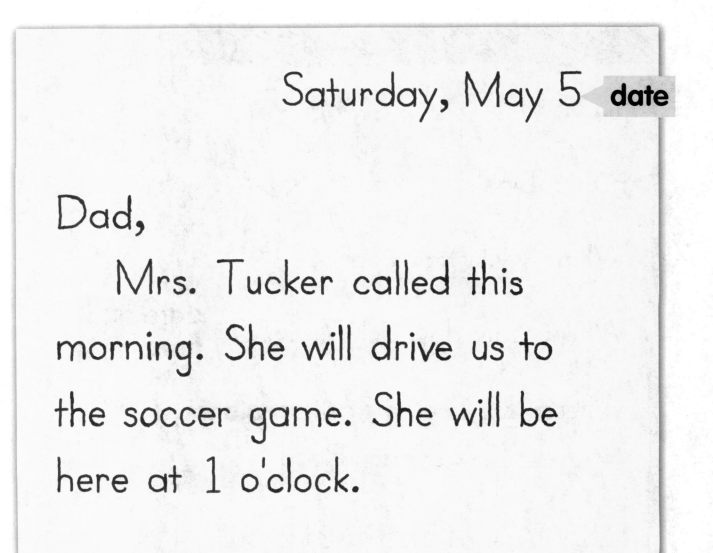

Saturday, May 5 — **date**

Dad,

    Mrs. Tucker called this morning. She will drive us to the soccer game. She will be here at 1 o'clock.

your name — Lily

Letters and Notes

Invitation

An **invitation** asks someone
to do something fun.

To: Sari

From: Daniel

What: My birthday party!

When: Saturday, July 7, 1:00   **date and time**

Where: Ice Cream Castle   **place**
726 Garden Road

R.S.V.P.: Call 555-3212
if you can come.

Thank-you Note

Write a **thank-you note** when someone gives you a gift.

greeting

July 10 date

Dear Sari,

Thank you for the crayons.
I really like them! I used them
to draw this picture of you.
Thank you for coming to
my birthday party.

closing Your friend,

your name Daniel

List

A **list** helps you remember things.

Things I Need for School

- ✓ lunch
- ✓ pencils
- ✓ math homework
- ✓ gym shoes
- ✓ milk carton for art project
- ✓ library book

Nonfiction Article

A **nonfiction article** tells about something that is true.

A Prickly Plant   title

A cactus is a plant.   topic

It grows in hot, dry places.   fact

It has thick skin and sharp needles. One kind of cactus is the saguaro. Its long branches look like arms. The saguaro can be 60 feet tall!

Paragraph

A **paragraph** is a group of sentences about one main idea.

indent

Winter is my favorite time of

year. I love the cold, fresh air.

I love to build snowmen. I love

to ice skate. I also like to stay

inside and drink hot cider!

main idea sentence

detail sentence

Poem

A **poem** has special words
in a special pattern.

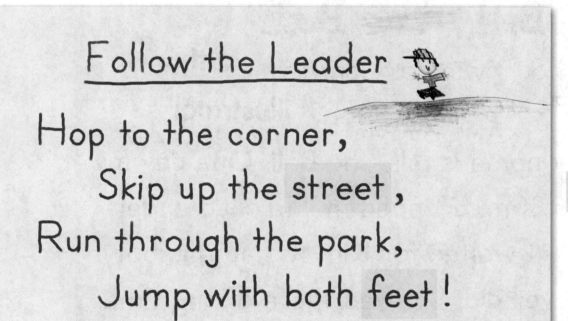

Follow the Leader

Hop to the corner,
  Skip up the street ,
Run through the park,
  Jump with both feet !

rhyme

In the Field

Three yellow flowers
Brighten up the cloudy day
Like tiny gold suns.

no rhyme

Story

A **story** can be real or make-believe.

Billy the Ball

Story by Tomás Gonzales   **author**

Pictures by Shoko Ito   **illustrator**

My name is Billy the Ball. One day my owner, Kim, dropped me. I rolled under a bush. I waited for Kim to find me, but she never did. I stayed there a long time.

One day a dog named Sparky found me. He pulled me out with his teeth. It hurt a little, but I was happy. He saved me! Now we play with Kim all the time.

Think of Questions

What do you want to learn about? Write questions.

> What is a real giant panda like?

The Giant Panda **topic**

1. Where does it live?

2. What does it eat?

3. What does it look like?

4. Is it scary?

Find Information

Use a Dictionary

A **dictionary** tells the meaning of words. It lists them in **alphabetical order**.

Nn

nest A bird lives in a nest.

nose You smell with your nose.

Oo

orange An orange is a fruit.

Pp

panda A panda is a big animal.

pencil You write with a pencil.

A B C D E F G H I J K L M N O P Q R S T U V W X Y Z

Look and Ask

Look at pictures.

Read words.

Ask people.

A Trip to the Library

You can find information in a **library**.

CD-ROMs

librarian

audiotapes

videotapes

books

magazines

Parts of a Book

These pages are at the beginning of a book.

Title Page

ANIMAL FACTS — title

by María Hernández — author

publisher — Better Books Inc.
Chicago, Illinois

Table of Contents

CONTENTS

page number

chapter title

More Parts of a Book

These pages are at the end.

Glossary

Dd

den a place where bears sleep

duck a bird that lives in the water

duckling a baby duck

42

meaning   **Ee**

ear the part of the body animals hear with

egg something that baby birds hatch from

elephant a very big animal with a long nose

43

Index

cat, 7–9, 36

claw, 5, 8

den, 22

duck, 10, 34

duckling, 34

52

ear, 4, 9, 12, 17

egg, 34, 37

elephant, 4, 38   **page numbers**

feathers, 10, 14

fox, 6, 22

53

Use a Computer

screen

icon

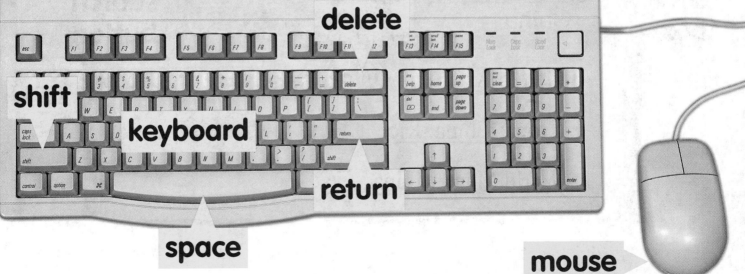

delete

shift

keyboard

return

space

mouse

Use the Internet

Look for information about
your topic. Follow these steps.

1. Click on the **Internet** icon.

2. Type your topic in the **search box**.

3. Click on the **search button**.

4. Click on a **Web site**.

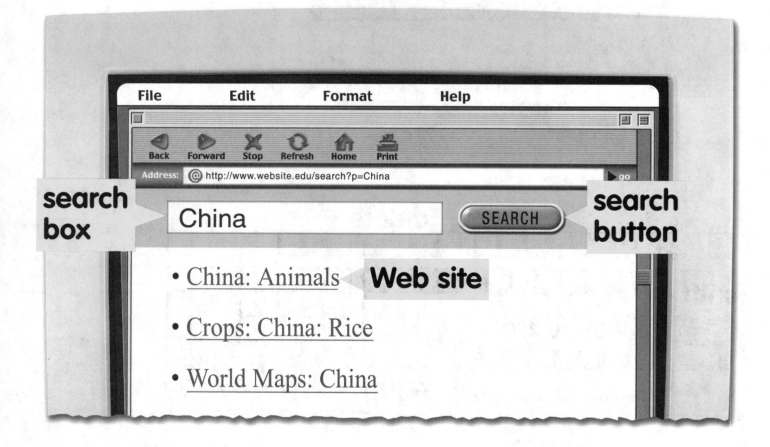

search box

search button

Web site